How the book is laid out – many of the [...]
and will be straightforward to identify using [...]
similarities and differences will be included [...]

*Curr[...]
evid[...]*

STAT[...]
*has [...]
Vuln[...]*

FLO[...]

HEIGHT *Check size*

DESCRIPTION *Check flowerspike shape, flower colour, shape, scent, check leaves*

HABITAT *Does it favour beechwoods, wetland or grassland?*

WHERE TO LOOK *Sites are named where possible but exact locations are not given where orchids grow on private land or when access is restricted.*

SIMILAR SPECIES *Key differences are described*

DID YOU KNOW? *Extra fact about the species*

Example –
Common Spotted-rchid

Types of orchid flower – each British orchid flower is made up of three sepals and three petals but one petal is usually dramatically different from the others and forms the lip. This is often brightly coloured, decorated with markings and elaborately shaped. The lip is actually the highest petal but it often lies at the base of the flower because either the ovary or its stalk has twisted. Flower shape, colour and markings can differ radically from one orchid to the next, sometimes within the same genus.

Violet Helleborine
Sepal
Petal — Petal
Sepal
Sepal
Lip (petal)
Pollinia

Common Twayblade
Ovary
Petals and sepals forming a hood
Sepal
Petals
Sepals
Bract
Lip (petal)

Green-winged Orchid
Spur
Petals and sepals forming a hood
Lip (petal)

Bee Orchid
Sepal
Petal
Petal
Pollinia
Sepal
Sepal
Lip (petal)

Hampshire and the Isle of Wight are home to 36 species of orchid, making it one of the best areas in Britain – what better place to start looking. Orchids can be found in chalk grassland, meadows, fens, marshes and woodland. These habitats, and some of the best places to look locally, are described here.

Grassland and heathland

The chalk grasslands of Hampshire and the Isle of Wight are some of the richest areas for orchids. Many of the rarer species can be found here like the Musk (pictured left), Frog and Burnt Orchids as well as some of the more common species like the Common Spotted-orchid, Pyramidal (pictured right), Chalk-fragrant and Bee Orchids. The New Forest holds the largest areas of heathland – look for Heath Spotted-orchid and Autumn Lady's-tresses.

WHERE TO LOOK Hants: Broughton Down, Butser Hill, Magdalen Hill Down, Martin Down, Noar Hill, Old Winchester Hill, Porton Down, St Catherine's Hill. **Isle of Wight**: Arreton Down, Compton Down, Knighton Down, Tennyson Down.

Woodland

Broadleaved woodland holds fewer orchid species than grassland, but the grassy woodland rides can be good places to look for Common Twayblade, Common Spotted-orchid and Early-purple Orchid. Hampshire's beechwoods however, are the places to head to for woodland helleborines, like Violet Helleborine (pictured), White Helleborine and the rare Narrow-leaved Helleborine. Bird's-nest Orchid and Fly Orchid favour these woodlands too.

WHERE TO LOOK Chappetts Copse and the beechwoods near Petersfield, Coulters Dean, Old Winchester Hill woodland, Shutts Copse, The Warren, Zebon Copse.

Wetland

Wetlands – marshes and fens are less well-represented in the region. These wetlands are home to Marsh Helleborine and the marsh-orchids like the Southern Marsh-orchid in particular. The Narrow-leaved Marsh-orchid is a rare fenland species. Bogs are confined mainly to the New Forest where the rare Bog Orchid still survives at a number of sites. Heath Spotted-orchid and Early Marsh-orchid subsp. *pulchella* (pictured) can also be seen.

WHERE TO LOOK Greywell Moors, Mapledurwell Fen, Winnall Moors. Matley Bog, Holmsley Bog and Wilverley Bog, Stony Cross and Hatchet Pond (all in the New Forest)

White Helleborine
Cephalanthera damasonium

STATUS Red Listing: Vulnerable. On Biodiversity Action Plan.

FLOWERING TIME Mid-May to early July

HEIGHT 15–45cm

DESCRIPTION This distinctive plant has broad, spear-shaped leaves that become narrower and shorter towards the top of the stem below upward-pointing, creamy-white flowers. With egg-shaped blooms that rarely open fully, it doesn't much resemble an orchid at first glance. Like other *Cephalanthera* helleborines, its flowers are much simpler than the more familiar orchid flower shape. The White Helleborine is usually self-pollinating, although pollination by insects has also been recorded. Though this plant takes at least eight years to develop from seed, and flowering can take an additional two to three years after that, it can spread to recently disturbed ground. It is one of our more common helleborines.

HABITAT The White Helleborine can be found in beech woodland on chalky soils. It is a shade-loving woodland species and is often the only plant found growing in clumps under the dense shade of beech trees. From time to time you can also find them under scrub and in more open grassland.

WHERE TO LOOK The beech woods in central and east Hampshire. Chappetts Copse managed by the Hampshire & Isle of Wight Wildlife Trust (HIWWT). The Warren National Nature Reserve (NNR) part of Ashford Hangers near Petersfield. In the woodlands at Old Winchester Hill (NNR), near Warnford.

DID YOU KNOW?

It is the barely visible yellow/orange lip of each flower that gives rise to its folk name 'poached egg plant'.

6

Narrow-leaved Helleborine
Cephalanthera longifolia

STATUS Red Listing: Vulnerable and Nationally Scarce. On the Biodiversity Action Plan UK list of priority species.

FLOWERING TIME Mid-May to early July

HEIGHT 20–50cm

DESCRIPTION The Narrow-leaved Helleborine is a regal plant with elegant, long leaves alternating all the way up the stem towards a leafless spire of pretty, pure white, bell-shaped flowers. Each flower has pointed sepals and opens just enough to reveal a golden patch on the heart-shaped lip. Each flower has a narrow, green bract. The seven to 20 leaves are fresh green in colour, strap-shaped and keeled with obvious veins. These thin, stiff leaves are 45cm long, giving rise to its alternative name, the Sword-leaved Helleborine. The flowers do not have a scent and the plant depends on bees and wasps for pollination.

HABITAT Locally this orchid is found in beechwoods, often with a fairly open canopy, but sometimes in deep shade. Sadly, it is found in less than 20 sites across England and numbers of plants are continuing to decline, making it one of our most threatened orchids. This is largely because of changes in woodland management.

WHERE TO LOOK This Hampshire speciality can be found at a few sites in the east of the county. Chappetts Copse nature reserve is considered a national stronghold and the local Wildlife Trust provides viewing areas where you can take pictures without endangering the plants.

SIMILAR SPECIES

White Helleborine (p.4) has creamier coloured flowers and its leaves are shorter and blunter. The bracts are also longer.

Red Helleborine
Cephalanthera rubra

STATUS Red Listing: Critically Endangered, Nationally Rare. Fully protected under Schedule 8 of the Wildlife and Countryside Act 1981.

FLOWERING TIME Early June to late July

HEIGHT 30–50cm

DESCRIPTION Arranged alternately on a wavy stem, the beautiful bell-like flowers of the Red Helleborine are closer to pink than red. When fully open the lateral sepals spread wide like outstretched arms. The stem is dusky-green, tinted purple towards the tip and sometimes with violet sheaths at the base. The flowers do not produce nectar but small, solitary bees are attracted to the sticky stigma.

HABITAT The Red Helleborine is a nationally rare and critically endangered woodland orchid that has been on the brink of extinction for the last 30 years. It only grows in three locations in Britain – Buckinghamshire, Gloucestershire and Hampshire. It is a delicate and fussy plant, and requires exactly the right habitat with the right mix of light and shade. Confined to calcareous soil, it prefers the ground under steeply sloping beech woodland where little else grows. However, too much shade will prevent it from flowering.

WHERE TO LOOK Locally the Red Helleborine is found at a single site in east Hampshire. The exact location is not widely advertised to protect the plant and to prevent thieves from digging up the orchid. (Unfortunately this has happened at some orchid sites in the past.)

DID YOU KNOW?

Though the Red Helleborine is extremely rare in Britain it grows throughout Europe and also occurs in Morocco, Algeria, Tunisia and parts of Southern Asia.

Marsh Helleborine
Epipactis palustris

FLOWERING TIME July and August

HEIGHT Up to 50cm

DESCRIPTION This showy and conspicuous orchid is easily identified by its colourful white and purple flowers, arranged in loose clusters, facing more or less to one side, attached to a reddish stem. The frilly white lip with purple veins at the base contrasts strikingly with a yellow column and reddish sepals that resemble wings. The Marsh Helleborine is cross-pollinated by a wide variety of insects including bees, beetles, flies, ants and spiders. The slightly hairy stalks and stem clasping leaves arise from an underground rhizome which is an effective method of asexual reproduction. Broader leaves grow at the base of the stem becoming narrower further up. The relatively large seeds which float on water enable the plant to colonise new areas.

HABITAT Marsh Helleborines favour wet, marshy habitats, including spring-fed fens, as well as seasonally flooded meadows. However, this orchid has declined substantially across the UK due to habitat loss, through land drainage and the enrichment of ground water in fertiliser run-off.

WHERE TO LOOK It is widespread but very local in Hampshire where suitable habitat occurs such as Greywell Moors and Mapledurwell Fen in north Hampshire (both HIWWT) and Luccombe on the Isle of Wight.

DID YOU KNOW?

The Marsh Helleborine is also found in wet dune slacks (seasonally flooded areas found next to sand dunes) around the coast. In this habitat it is usually shorter and stockier than those found inland.

Violet Helleborine
Epipactis purpurata

FLOWERING TIME Late July to September

HEIGHT Up to 100cm

DESCRIPTION Though closely related to the Broad-leaved Helleborine, the flowers of the Violet Helleborine are less variable and are greenish-white in colour. The inner cup-shaped part of the lip is purple on the inside and white on the outside. The stem and the leaves are a dull, greyish-green, sometimes tinted purple. It is one of the last orchids to come into flower. The Violet Helleborine is cross-pollinated by wasps and the nectar is thought to have a narcotic effect. Visiting insects become sluggish and may even drop to the ground. It is a long-lived orchid: a single-stemmed plant may be 30 years old and multi-stemmed plants are thought to be hundreds of years old.

HABITAT Violet Helleborines prefer shade and are usually found in woodland, in deep shade where little else can grow. They can also be found on roadside verges close to woodland. Nationally these plants have declined over the last 150 years as ancient woodlands have been destroyed or replanted with conifers.

WHERE TO LOOK Apart from a few outlying populations in west-central and southern Hampshire, they can be found mainly in the chalk woodlands between Petersfield and Basingstoke, in small populations. The village of Four Marks near Alton in east Hampshire is considered a stronghold for the Violet Helleborine where it can be found along several road-verges.

DID YOU KNOW?
Of all the woodland helleborines, the Violet Helleborine has the brightest flowers. It gets its name not from the flower colour, but from its leaves, which are often tinged purple.

14

Broad-leaved Helleborine
Epipactis helleborine

FLOWERING TIME July to September

HEIGHT Up to 100cm

DESCRIPTION As the name suggests, the leaves of this sturdy plant are broad, especially lower down, with obvious veins or pleats. Plants can grow up to one metre in height with as many as 100 individual flowers. However, the flowers are relatively subtle in size and colour and blend well into the background making them surprisingly tricky to spot. The flowers can vary enormously from entirely green or purple to a mixture of pale green, violet, pink and purple. The sepals are triangular-oval, quite large and pale green, becoming paler towards the edges. The petals are smaller, whitish or pinkish, becoming greener to the centre. The flowers are mildly scented. The Broad-Leaved Helleborine is cross-pollinated by small wasps, especially long-headed species and, similar to the Violet Helleborine, the nectar has a narcotic effect.

HABITAT This is the most common and widespread of the helleborines and grows in and around deciduous woodlands, particularly beechwoods. It prefers the brighter areas in glades and along the woodland edge so you might also stumble across it along a shady lane, a roadside verge, or railway cutting. The Broad-leaved Helleborine can also grow in deep shade.

WHERE TO LOOK It is a widely distributed and sometimes abundant orchid at good sites throughout Hampshire, such as Butser Hill and Zebon Copse next to Basingstoke Canal, both managed by Hampshire County Council (HCC). Coulters Dean (HIWWT) and The Warren (NNR).

SIMILAR SPECIES

Violet Helleborine (p.12) and Narrow-lipped Helleborine (p.16) both prefer the shadier conditions of beech woodland.

Narrow-lipped Helleborine
Epipactis leptochila

STATUS Red Listing: Nationally Scarce

FLOWERING TIME Mid-July to early August

HEIGHT Up to 75cm

DESCRIPTION Closely related to the Broad-leaved Helleborine, the Narrow-lipped Helleborine has drooping flowers which are yellow-green to olive-green in colour with never any trace of violet or purple. The well-spaced flowers are always wide open but unlike its close cousin, it is a self-pollinating plant. The pale green ovaries are prominently six-ribbed but not twisted. The outer part of the lip appears long, narrow and pointed, hence the common name and is held projecting prominently outwards. The stems, which grow singly are noticeably hairy, and bear two rows of veined, fresh green leaves. The base of the stalk is also greenish-yellow.

HABITAT Beechwoods are the favoured habitat of this scarce and local orchid which loves deep shade where there is little or no ground cover. (It cannot tolerate direct sunlight.)

WHERE TO LOOK The Narrow-lipped Helleborine is one of the rarest of the *Epipactis* group of helleborines to be found in Hampshire. It only grows in a few locations, including a possible site at Aldersbrook near Headley. It does not occur on the Isle of Wight.

SIMILAR SPECIES

The Narrow-lipped Helleborine is closely related to the Broad-leaved Helleborine (p.14) but the flowers have pointed lips rather than rounded lips. It was not until 1921 that Narrow-leaved Helleborine was described as a separate species.

Green-flowered Helleborine
Epipactis phyllanthes

STATUS Red Listing: Nationally Scarce

FLOWERING TIME July to early October

HEIGHT Up to 40cm

DESCRIPTION The Green-flowered Helleborine is one of the most variable orchids and can cause quite a bit of confusion when trying to identify it because it appears in many different shapes and sizes. Typically it has a relatively slender stem and the upper part is hairless and sometimes leafless. When leaves are present they are short and rounded, often with wavy edges and are bright apple-green in colour. The mass of light green flowers droop downwards and often do not open at all. This species appears to rely entirely on self-pollination and it is probably the resulting inbreeding which has led to the diversity of the plant.

HABITAT This is a mysterious woodland orchid and has a habit of appearing and disappearing from known sites and popping up in unexpected places. It is found in beechwoods and a variety of other woodlands, with chalky and sandy soils in both wet and dry conditions. Colonies are often small and numbers can fluctuate, with fewer plants in dry years.

WHERE TO LOOK Hampshire is the centre of distribution for this species in southern England. It is widespread but local, with several sites throughout the county, most often in central and northern Hampshire, including the southern part of Winnall Moors (HIWWT) and areas in the river valleys of the Test and Itchen. Plants have also been recorded in Tadley and Middle Wallop.

DID YOU KNOW?

The Green-flowered Helleborine is also known as the Pendulous-flowered Helleborine.

20

Common Twayblade

Neottia ovata

FLOWERING TIME Mid-May to early August

HEIGHT Up to 45cm

DESCRIPTION With a tall spike of small, green flowers this unassuming plant is often camouflaged against a backdrop of fresh spring greenery of the woodland floor or tall downland grasses. The petals and sepals form a hood-like structure which is green with some purple patterning. A long green, strap-like lip hangs downwards and divides into two (bilobed) and holds a channel of nectar that acts like a landing strip for visiting wasps, sawflies and beetles. Attracted by the musk scent of the flowers, these insects crawl up the lip following the nectar channel and the pollinia become stuck onto the insect's body by the sudden release of a drop of sticky liquid which the insect inadvertently triggers. This method of using insects as pollinators is extremely effective and most flowers will set seed. It is also a very long-lived plant. The Common Twayblade gets its name from the pair of large, oval leaves held opposite each other at the base of the stem.

HABITAT Twayblades are common and well-known in the UK. They are not fussy plants and will grow in profusion in open woodland, downland, fens and at the edge of arable fields. They can also be found in relatively new habitats, such as sandpits, quarries and disused railway lines.

WHERE TO LOOK Widespread and frequent throughout the region. One of Hampshire's commonest orchids. You can see Common Twayblade in the scrub at Old Winchester Hill (NNR) and Noar Hill (HIWWT), as well as on roadside verges in the New Forest, and in ancient woodlands.

SIMILAR SPECIES

Man Orchid (p.56) and Frog Orchid (p.40) also have greenish flowers, though the structure of the lip is very different. See p.70 for Lesser Twayblade.

Bird's-nest Orchid

Neottia nidus-avis

STATUS Red Listing: Near Threatened

FLOWERING TIME Mid-May to early July

HEIGHT Up to 45cm, usually 20–40cm

DESCRIPTION The honey-brown flower spikes of the Bird's-nest Orchid are unique among wild British orchids. Most of the flowers are clustered together towards the tip of the stem, becoming more widely spaced with one or two odd flowers further down the stem. Typical of an orchid flower, the petals and sepals form a loose hood and the lip vaguely resembles a human torso. The flowers are dominated by the large, slightly darker lip which has outward hanging lobes and a nectar-producing depression at the base. For those with a keen sense of smell, the flowers have a mild, honey-like scent. These flowers are pollinated by insects, including flies, attracted by the nectar. The leaves are stunted and brown and the whole plant has the look of a withered winter stem from the previous year. This orchid is sustained by a living fungus. It forms a relationship with ectomycorrhizal fungi which are simultaneously in partnership with nearby trees.

HABITAT Though rather scarce and local, the Bird's-Nest Orchid is reasonably widespread in the heavy shade of mature beech woods on limestone soils. Because they are so inconspicuous this species may well be under-recorded.

WHERE TO LOOK Head for the chalk of central Hampshire, ancient woodlands such as Chappetts Copse, Shutts Copse (HIWWT) and Zebon Copse (HCC), the woodland at Old Winchester Hill (NNR), as well as Porton Down on the Wiltshire/ Hampshire border. It is also frequently found in the New Forest.

DID YOU KNOW?

The Bird's-nest Orchid takes it name from its mass of peculiar, short, thick roots said to resemble a bird's nest.

Bog Orchid
Hammarbya paludosa

FLOWERING TIME July to mid-September

HEIGHT 3–12cm

DESCRIPTION The Bog Orchid is Britain's smallest native orchid and it is not an easy species to see. They rarely grow taller than 8cm, the angular stems are pale and the flowers too are an understated yellow/green. There are usually up to 15 flowers, just 3mm long. In contrast to other orchid flowers, those of the Bog Orchid appear upside-down so that the lip points upwards. It is marked with subtle stripes of light and dark green, leading to a base that secretes nectar to attract pollinating insects, such as gnats, midges and small flies.

HABITAT True to its name the Bog Orchid is a speciality of wetland habitats. It often grows in the wettest, deepest, most inaccessible parts of valley mires, among floating carpets of sphagnum mosses. It is one of our most threatened and dramatically declining species largely because of the loss of vast areas of suitable wetland. The acid moorlands of the New Forest are one of the last major strongholds of this species in Europe.

WHERE TO LOOK This very scarce and local orchid can only be found in a few small populations in the New Forest, such as Matley, Holmsley and Wilverley Bogs, together with Stoney Cross, Hatchet Pond and Acres Down.

CAUTION

Bogs can be treacherous places, with vegetation concealing deep water beneath. Every care should be taken when visiting these sites.

26

Autumn Lady's-tresses

Spiranthes spiralis

STATUS Red Listing: Near Threatened

FLOWERING TIME Early August to late September

HEIGHT 10cm

DESCRIPTION This delicate and singular plant is our latest-flowering orchid. From a walking height it is easily missed so the best way to see it is to get down on your hands and knees and scan along the ground. With a pale green stem, this orchid has a slender spike with white, bell-shaped flowers arranged in a single row which usually follow a spiral pattern around the stem. It is the spiral of flowers resembling a lady's braided hair that lends the plant its name. It is pollinated by small solitary bees which visit the flowers soon after they have opened. Unlike other European orchids the leaves are all in a rosette at ground level – a growth which allows the orchid to thrive in such unlikely places as lawns and tennis courts.

HABITAT This species favours old, dry grasslands on sunny sites and a needs a short sward in which to grow as it is easily outcompeted by taller vegetation. Chalk downland and the heavily grazed 'lawns' of the New Forest are particularly suitable.

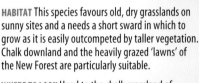

WHERE TO LOOK Head to the chalk grassland of St Catherine's Hill (HIWWT), Old Winchester Hill (NNR), and Butterfly Conservation's (BC) Magdalen Hill Down in central Hampshire. Further south, visit Portsdown Hill (HCC) in Portsmouth, or Knighton Down on the Isle of Wight (HIWWT). The New Forest also has lots of good sites including Wilverley Plain.

DID YOU KNOW?

Now declared extinct from Britain, the closely related Summer Lady's-tresses (p.70) was last recorded on a Hampshire site, in the more southerly part of the New Forest, near Lyndhurst, in the 1950s.

28

Musk Orchid

Herminium monorchis

STATUS Red Listing: Vulnerable and Nationally Scarce. On the Biodiversity Action Plan UK list of priority species.

FLOWERING TIME Early June to early July

HEIGHT Up to 15cm

DESCRIPTION The small, spiky-looking Musk Orchid is rather inconspicuous and easily overlooked and in some ways looks more like a lily than an orchid. The stem is yellowish-green to dark green and clearly ridged towards the tip. The lowest pair of mid-green leaves are much broader than the stem leaves which are bract-like. The tiny, angular, bell-like flowers are tightly clustered on the spike, with 20–30 flowers on most plants. Each flower is entirely greenish-yellow with a three-lobed lip which is hardly separated from the rest of the flower and the sepals and petals form a loose, tapering hood. The flowers do not open widely but have a subtle scent of musk or honey. They are pollinated by a variety of small insects such as flies, parasitic wasps, gnats and beetles, which crawl into the flowers and unwittingly pick up the sticky pollinia.

HABITAT The Musk Orchid is found on short, well-drained grassland on chalk or limestone. Because it is a small plant it cannot compete with taller vegetation. It has been lost from 69% of its historical range in the UK largely because of agricultural 'improvements' and the ploughing up of chalk grassland. It is particularly vulnerable to drought conditions and a hot, dry summer can cause a dramatic fall in the number of flowers the following year.

WHERE TO LOOK Noar Hill near Selborne in east Hampshire has a nationally important colony of Musk Orchids, though you need to get down on your hands and knees to scan for them. You can also see them on St Catherine's Hill in Winchester, (both HIWWT).

DID YOU KNOW?

With its shallow roots the Musk Orchid is highly sensitive to drought conditions. The heatwave in the summer of 1976 wiped out many populations.

Greater Butterfly-orchid
Platanthera chlorantha

FLOWERING TIME Mid-June until mid-August

HEIGHT 60cm

DESCRIPTION The larger of the two butterfly-orchids is an elegant plant with beautiful white or greenish-white flowers, often held on a tall spike. The pale green stem has two oval, shiny leaves growing from its base and becomes ribbed towards the tip. The flowers have a long, narrow lip and an exceptionally long, thin spur which is rich in nectar. After dusk the white flowers almost glow in the dark and emit a mild scent to attract night-flying hawkmoths. It is only an insect with a very long proboscis that can reach the nectar. As the moth sips from the spur, the pollinia become 'glued' to its proboscis, and the insect inadvertently cross-pollinates the plant.

HABITAT The Greater Butterfly-orchid prefers light, dappled shade and is usually found in more open areas along the edge of a woodland and in clearings beside rides. Plants tend to be shorter and more compact in these locations. It can also be found on chalk grassland, often in long grass. It can tolerate both wet and dry soils and is able to colonise recently disturbed ground.

WHERE TO LOOK In the north of Hampshire head to Porton Down on the Hants/Wiltshire border. Martin Down (NNR) to the far west, Yew Hill (BC) near Winchester and Old Winchester Hill (NNR) are also good sites.

31

SIMILAR SPECIES

The Greater Butterfly-orchid's pollinia are widely spaced and converge towards the top of the flower, whereas the similar Lesser Butterfly-orchid (p.32) has closely spaced, parallel pollinia.

Lesser Butterfly-orchid

Platanthera bifolia

STATUS Red Listing: Vulnerable. On the Biodiversity Action Plan UK list of priority species.

FLOWERING TIME June and July

HEIGHT Up to 45cm

DESCRIPTION Though very similar in appearance to its close relative, the Lesser Butterfly-orchid is more delicate and daintier with fewer, smaller flowers in a narrower spike. While it also has white flowers with a narrow lip and an extremely long spur, the mouth of the spur is narrower and the spur tends to be straighter. The main distinction however, is the arrangement of the pollinia, which lie closely parallel to each other. The flowers also have a headier carnation scent, more powerful than the perfume of its cousin. The Lesser Butterfly-orchid is also pollinated by night-flying moths, especially hawkmoths.

HABITAT This shy orchid is very local in the region and tends to hide beneath bracken in the acid grasslands of the New Forest. Occasionally it grows in the wetter fringes of bogs. In Hampshire it is much scarcer than the Greater Butterfly-orchid.

WHERE TO LOOK Though scarce and local in Hampshire, and occurring in small populations, the Lesser Butterfly-orchid is most frequently found on the higher, drier ground in and around bogs in the New Forest near Holmsley and near Beaulieu Road.

SIMILAR SPECIES

The Lesser Butterfly-orchid's pollinia are closely spaced and parallel, whereas the similar Greater Butterfly-orchid (p.30) has widely spaced pollinia that converge towards the top.

Chalk Fragrant-orchid
Gymnadenia conopsea

FLOWERING TIME Late May to late July

HEIGHT 15–45cm

DESCRIPTION This delicate and pretty orchid has a long, tall flower spike that varies in colour from shades of pink to reddish-purple and sometimes white. Each flower has two lateral sepals spread out horizontally with a 'rolled-up' appearance and a flat, three-lobed lip that lacks 'shoulders' with a long, slender, down-curved spur which is filled with nectar. The 20–50 flowers emit a spicy scent with a hint of carnation (it is sometimes described as a slightly unpleasant, rancid scent), which attracts both day- and night-flying moths and butterflies. Two long, ribbon-like leaves are found at the stalk base and the shorter leaves up the stem are strongly keeled.

HABITAT As the name suggests, the Chalk Fragrant-orchid grows in species-rich chalk grassland. It favours warm, dry and open locations such as chalk pits and downland. It once grew in large colonies but as downs and pastures have been turned into farmland, this is a less common occurrence.

WHERE TO LOOK Old Winchester Hill (NNR), Noar Hill and Coulters Dean (both HIWWT), Yew Hill (BC) and Martin Down (NNR) in the glades of Vernditch Chase. Arreton Down in Newport on the Isle of Wight (HIWWT). If you are lucky enough to visit a large colony, the perfume emitted by so many flowers can be quite powerful, particularly at dusk.

DID YOU KNOW?

The Chalk Fragrant-orchid is also known as the Common Fragrant-orchid. Since 1997, using new molecular and genetic data, the 'Fragrant Orchid' has been separated into three distinct species, Chalk, Marsh and Heath Fragrant-orchids.

Marsh Fragrant-orchid

Gymnadenia densiflora

STATUS Red Listing: Data Deficient

FLOWERING TIME Late June to mid-August

HEIGHT 30–60cm, can grow up to 100cm

DESCRIPTION Though closely related to the Chalk Fragrant-orchid looks quite different and is a much larger plant, almost twice the size. It has a more tightly packed flower spike with up to 100 dark pink flowers which are a slightly different shape. Though the lip is also broader than long, with three clearly defined lobes, it has obvious 'shoulders'. The lateral sepals are long and narrow with a blunt tip and are held out horizontally and there is a long, slender, down-curved spur from which butterflies and moths sip nectar. Unlike its close relation, the flowers of the Marsh Fragrant-orchid smell strongly of cloves. The basal rosette of leaves appears in autumn and lasts through the winter.

HABITAT The Marsh Fragrant-orchid grows exclusively on fenland sites and meadows fed by chalky water. These tall plants can be easy to spot in fens, although the habitat is very local. It has undergone a serious decline across much of the country because of the drainage and destruction of fen and marsh habitats.

WHERE TO LOOK Mapledurwell Fen (HIWWT) in north Hampshire supports many of the marsh orchids, including Marsh Fragrant-orchid. Areas of heathland and bog in the New Forest also support significant populations.

SIMILAR SPECIES

The Chalk Fragrant-orchid (p.34) is smaller and daintier than the Marsh Fragrant-orchid, though the Heath Fragrant-orchid (p.38) is the smallest of the three species.

38

Heath Fragrant-orchid

Gymnadenia borealis

STATUS Red Listing: Data Deficient

FLOWERING TIME Early June to end August

HEIGHT 10–15cm

DESCRIPTION Heath Fragant-orchid is the smallest of the three fragrant-orchids. The fairly open spikes are delicate with small flowers, varying in colour from pale mauve to dark pink. The lateral sepals are small, flat and pointed. The lip is small with two subtle side lobes and a longer central lobe. The spur is smaller than that of its two cousins. The flowers have a strong, sweet scent, similar to carnations, compared to the more spicy scent of the Marsh Fragrant-orchid or the sickly-sweet perfume of the Chalk Fragrant-orchid.

HABITAT This species is most commonly found on moorlands of northern England and Scotland. It is the only fragrant-orchid to regularly grow in acid soils. In Hampshire it is restricted to the New Forest where a few small populations can be found. It often grows in thick clumps of tussocky grass and heather and the delicate spikes can be difficult to spot.

WHERE TO LOOK Head to Stony Moors, Dibden Bottom and Roundway Hill in the New Forest.

SIMILAR SPECIES

The Chalk Fragrant-orchid (p.34) and the Marsh Fragrant-orchid (p.36) are larger and more commonly occurring than the Heath Fragrant-orchid.

Frog Orchid
Coeloglossum viride

FLOWERING TIME Early June to early August

HEIGHT Up to 25cm, usually much shorter

DESCRIPTION This diminutive orchid has an intriguing name and those with an active imagination may agree that the flowers vaguely resemble the hind legs of a frog. The flowers though are rather inconspicuous, and vary from green or yellowish-green to reddish-brown in colour. The sepals and petals form a protective hood over the extended, hanging three-pointed lip which is usually paler in colour. The faint-smelling flowers attract a variety of small insects, including beetles and wasps, which take the nectar from the short spur. The Frog Orchid is also known as the Long-bracted Green Orchid because the green, lower bracts can be up to twice as long as the flowers. It is a short-lived species, many plants die after just one year above ground.

HABITAT The Frog Orchid is locally frequent on chalk downland in central and north Hampshire, but rare on the Isle of Wight. It has become extinct in many counties across Britain due to habitat loss from the ploughing up of old pastures and the invasion of scrub and other more dominant plants.

WHERE TO LOOK Martin Down (NNR), Noar Hill, St Catherine's Hill, (HIWWT) and Old Winchester Hill (NNR) on the south-facing slopes. It is best to look for this species on your hands and knees and scanning the ground.

DID YOU KNOW?
The Man Orchid (p.56) and the Common Twayblade (p.20) have the same long and narrow 'arms' and 'legs' on the lip.

Common Spotted-orchid

Dactylorhiza fuchsii

FLOWERING TIME Late May to July

HEIGHT Up to 65cm

DESCRIPTION The Common Spotted-orchid is quite straightforward to identify. True to its name, it is both common and has clearly spotted leaves. The flowers form a pyramidal spike and are various shades of pink or lilac, and often very pale. The lateral sepals are asymmetrical and held horizontally, patterned with lines and spots. The lip is decorated with dark lines and loops and is divided into three lobes with a longer and more triangular central lobe. The green leaves are usually marked with solid, dark spots all over. A wide variety of insects cross-pollinate this species, including beetles. The orchid does not however produce nectar, so the insects are duped into visiting the mildly scented flowers.

HABITAT This is our most common and widespread orchid and is found in a variety of habitats including open, dry grassland, damp fen and woodland, along rides, clearings and edges. It can colonise new areas fairly easily, including roadside and railway verges and can appear in large numbers. However, within the same population the plants can vary enormously.

WHERE TO LOOK Up to 20,000 Common Spotted-orchids were recently recorded at Coulters Dean (HIWWT) above the village of Buriton in the South Downs. Martin Down (NNR), Butser Hill (HCC), Yew Hill (BC), Noar Hill (HIWWT), Dundridge nature reserve (HCC) and Beacon Hill near Warnford.

SIMILAR SPECIES

The Early-purple Orchid (p.52) also has spotted leaves but the lip is a very different shape and does not have bold darker lines and loops. It also flowers earlier in the spring. Heath Spotted-orchid (p.44) is very similar but the lip is wider, the lobes are different sizes and the markings are more delicate.

Heath Spotted-orchid

Dactylorhiza maculata

FLOWERING PERIOD Late May to July

HEIGHT 10–25cm

DESCRIPTION The graceful stalks of the Heath Spotted-orchid bear attractive flowers that are closely clustered together. Flower colour varies from white to purplish pink and patterned with darker fine dots and dashes. Unlike its close relation, the Common Spotted-orchid, this species has a lip that resembles a wide petticoat and the side-lobes are much wider than the very small central lobe. The flowers are faintly scented and cross-pollinated by numerous insects including bees and flies. The lower leaves are tongue-shaped with a blunt point while the upper leaves are pointed. All leaves have small, dull purplish-brown spots.

HABITAT The Heath Spotted-orchid is one of the few British orchids that prefers acid soils. It is the most common of the New Forest orchids and is abundant and widespread throughout much of the area. New Forest specimens are usually significantly shorter than national plants and sometimes have a dense, conical spike of pale pink flowers clustered around the tip.

WHERE TO LOOK The heaths of north-east Hampshire around Farnborough and Aldershot including the wetter parts of Tadley Common and Whitehouse Meadow (HIWWT). Many of the heaths in the New Forest.

SIMILAR SPECIES

Common Spotted-orchid (p.42) which has bigger, bolder spots on the leaves. The lip is also more deeply lobed and the spur is shorter and thicker.

Early Marsh-orchid
Dactylorhiza incarnata

FLOWERING TIME Late May to early July

HEIGHT Up to 50cm

DESCRIPTION There are five subspecies of Early Marsh-orchid, each with a different distribution in Britain. The subspecies *incarnata* (pictured left) has typically flesh pink flowers that can vary from white to purplish-pink. The sepals are held upward and resemble donkey's ears, often with dark pink speckles and sometimes ring-shaped patterns. The upper sepal and petals form a tight hood above a furrowed lip that has dark loop markings. It is slightly lobed with the sides turned downwards. The subspecies *pulchella* (pictured below) is the commonest of the group found in Hampshire. The flowers are a deep magenta-red with even darker loop-shaped markings. The lip is usually entire (not three-lobed) with a rounded diamond shape and appears flat. In both cases, as there is no nectar, the naïve, early-flying bumblebees are tricked into visiting the flowers. The *Dactylorhiza* marsh-orchids are all extremely variable in both shape and colour. This diversity is caused partly by a striking ability to hybridise within the genus.

HABITAT The Early Marsh-orchid (subspecies *incarnata*) is usually found in marshes, fens and waterside meadows in small numbers at scattered sites throughout central and north-east Hampshire. The subspecies *pulchella* is a plant of sphagnum bogs in the New Forest, where it is widespread. Like many other wetland species marsh-orchids are becoming scarce because of land drainage and the agricultural 'improvement' of their habitats. It has gone from over 40% of its historical range in Britain.

WHERE TO LOOK The Warren (NNR) near Petersfield and the heaths around the Surrey/Hants border. Warnborough Greens in north Hants (HIWWT). Bogs in the New Forest.

SIMILAR SPECIES

Southern Marsh-orchid (p.48) is a similar but much larger plant, with larger flowers that are also a darker pink.

48

Southern Marsh-orchid
Dactylorhiza pratermissa

FLOWERING TIME June to mid-July

HEIGHT Up to 70cm

DESCRIPTION This distinctive plant is tall with a strong stem and a crowded, cylindrical spike of pale pink to deep red-violet flowers. Each flower has a prominent saucer-shaped lip centrally marked with speckles and dashes. Though it is very variable, and some plants can be more intense in colour, most flowers appear slightly faded. The vaguely circular lip has three subtle lobes including a small tooth-like central lobe which points forwards. The spur is thick, slightly curved and tapering. There are several broad, spear-shaped, grey-green leaves which are usually unmarked.

HABITAT The Southern Marsh-orchid often grows in large colonies which can stand out but single plants can be trickier to spot. Locally common, it prefers very wet soils. Typical habitats include marshes, water meadows or fens along the river valleys throughout Hampshire and the Isle of Wight. It can also be seen along roadside verges. It is the most common of the marsh-orchids in the two counties.

WHERE TO LOOK In and around valley mires in the New Forest. Other sites include Martin Down (NNR), Greywell Moors, Mapledurwell Fen, Bramshill Common at Sand Pit Pond, Southmoor and Warnborough Greens, the northern part of Winnall Moors (all HIWWT sites).

SIMILAR SPECIES

The flower spike of the Early Marsh-orchid (p.46) is usually a paler, fleshier pink with smaller flowers that have a narrower lip with obvious double-loop markings. The Northern Marsh-orchid (p.71) has a more densely packed, square-topped spike.

Narrow-leaved Marsh-orchid
Dactylorhiza traunsteinerioides

STATUS Red Listing: Nationally Scarce

FLOWERING TIME Late May to late July

HEIGHT 20–40cm

DESCRIPTION This nationally scarce orchid is one of the first marsh-orchids to come into flower and it is the most localised. It is also known as Pugley's Marsh-orchid, first found in Ireland by H. W. Pugsley. In contrast to the Southern Marsh-orchid it has a thin, weak stem with a few ribbon-like leaves that are often twisted and unspotted. The short, loose flower spike just has a few large, pale red-purple flowers, giving the species a more delicate appearance than other marsh orchids. The flowers all roughly face in one direction. The lip has a characteristic triangular shape and is marked with dark dots, dashes and squiggles which often extend to the edges. It has three lobes with a long, protruding central lobe. The spur is quite long and robust looking. The plant freely hybridises with other species, including the Southern Marsh-orchid, and in some locations the hybrids are much more common than the pure species.

HABITAT The Narrow-leaved Marsh-orchid needs very specific conditions to flourish. It grows in the wettest areas among rushes and sedges, rooting in the mossy layer at the base of other vegetation.

WHERE TO LOOK In this region it is confined to only two established sites in Hampshire, one on a small fenland reserve near Basingstoke, Mapledurwell Fen and The Hatch (HIWWT), the other on the eastern edge of the New Forest.

SIMILAR SPECIES

Early Marsh-orchid (p.46) has different markings on the lip and broader leaves. The Southern Marsh-orchid (p.48) is taller and stronger with a larger flower spike and usually many more flowers.

Early-purple Orchid

Orchis mascula

FLOWERING TIME Early April to late May

HEIGHT Up to 40cm

DESCRIPTION The Early-purple Orchid is our earliest flowering species and with its tall, purple flower spikes and spotted leaves, identification is straightforward. The oval spike is open and irregular in shape with ten to 50 flowers in various shades of purple. The upper sepal and petals form a loose hood over the column and the two lateral sepals are held upwards and backwards like angel's wings. The three-lobed lip points downwards and outwards and often has a crease running through the centre. The flowers emit a strong smell of cat's urine to attract visiting bumblebees and solitary bees, though the plant does not produce nectar. *Orchis* means testicle and beneath an Early-purple Orchid is a pair of testicle-like root-tubers; one withers as it powers the plant, the other develops for next year's growth. The Hampshire name Adder's Flower celebtates the appearance of the flowers when the first adders also begin to emerge.

HABITAT The Early-purple Orchid is generally common and easy to find throughout the two counties, although most populations consist of small numbers. It grows in ancient and coppiced woodland where they are often found alongside bluebells, primroses and wood anemones. You may also find this species in rough pasture and open downland, as well as meadows, railway embankments and road verges.

WHERE TO LOOK Martin Down (NNR), Noar Hill (HIWWT) and Butser Hill (HCC). Tennyson Down, towards the Needles and Compton Down on the south coast of the Isle of Wight.

SIMILAR SPECIES

Although similar, the Green-winged Orchid (p.62) has green veins on its sepals and doesn't have the outstretched wings of the Early-purple Orchid. The Green-winged Orchid always has unspotted leaves and does not grow in woodland.

54

Lady Orchid
Orchis purpurea

STATUS Red Listing: Endangered and Nationally Scarce

FLOWERING TIME Early May to early June

HEIGHT Up to 100cm

DESCRIPTION The Lady Orchid is a stately plant with up to 50 large flowers clustered in an oval spike. The sepals and upper petals form a hood, coloured by dense parallel lines and dark reddish-brown flecks, which creates the 'Lady's bonnet'. The wide, three-lobed lip is shaped like a little figure wearing a crinoline gown. The lip is white or pale pink, speckled with dark red dots which are caused by groups of coloured hairs. Both the leaves and flowers smell of new-mown hay. The shiny green, unspotted leaves are very robust. The plant is pollinated by small digger wasps and bumblebees.

HABITAT The Lady Orchid prefers open woodland on shallow, well-drained chalky soil. It is happiest in well-lit areas along paths and rides but requires shelter from the wind. It is nationally scarce and has vanished from 57% of its historical range. Loss of woodlands and lack of coppicing have been major factors, but rabbits and slugs have also played a part in this plant's decline.

WHERE TO LOOK This orchid is only found on one site in Hampshire, in a small colony on the Wiltshire/Hants border at Porton Down. Growing in the woodland it is not as leafy and stout as chalk downland specimens. It also has darker flowers.

SIMILAR SPECIES

The Burnt Orchid (p.58), found on chalk grassland, is a similar colour with a dark hood and a white lip with purple spots, but is tiny by comparison.

56

Man Orchid

Orchis anthropophora

STATUS Red Listing: Nationally Scarce. On the Biodiversity Action Plan UK list of priority species.

FLOWERING TIME Mid-May to June

HEIGHT Up to 40cm

DESCRIPTION The long, thin spikes of the Man Orchid are characteristic of the plant. The flowers are pale yellowish to brownish-green in colour with copper-brown, deeply lobed lips. Each bloom closely resembles a tiny figure: the sepals and petals form a 'head' that faces downwards and the lip forms the dangling 'arms' and 'legs'. The flowers have a faint, unpleasant smell and open gradually from the bottom of the spike. There is no spur but two small depressions at the base of the lip produce the nectar which attracts a variety of insects, including ants and hoverflies. The lower leaves are very broad, tongue-shaped and clearly veined with rounded ends but the uppermost leaves are pointed and encircle the stem.

HABITAT This species favours well-drained grassland and scrub on chalk and limestone soils including open banks and the lower slopes of hillsides. It can sometimes be found in old abandoned chalk pits and limestone quarries.

WHERE TO LOOK The Man Orchid is now a very rare species in Hampshire and only occurs in a small number of sites including Martin Down and Old Winchester Hill (both NNRs). It was last recorded on the Isle of Wight in the 1970s.

SIMILAR SPECIES

The Frog Orchid (p.40) is a similar colour but is smaller and the lip is not divided into 'arms' and 'legs'. Common Twayblade (p.20) is also similar but it only has two large leaves held opposite each other.

58

Burnt Orchid
Neotinea ustulata

STATUS Red Listing: Nationally Scarce

FLOWERING TIME Mid-May to July

HEIGHT 5–20cm

DESCRIPTION This small plant is one of our more striking orchids and it is easy to identify. The compact flower spike has small, dark unopened buds that contrast dramatically with the white lips of the opened flowers, giving the top of the spike a scorched or burnt appearance. It is one of the manikin orchids in which the flower resembles a tiny human figure, with the lobes of the lip becoming the 'arms' and 'legs'. The petals form a helmet which is initially brown-violet later turning bright red. The lip is marked with regularly spaced red dots and a groove along the centre towards the base that leads to the short, down-curved spur. The strongly and sweetly scented flowers attract pollinating insects including flies which approach the flowers upside-down, possibly the only way they can access the narrow mouth of the spur. A rosette of two to five green oblong, keeled leaves grow at the base of the stem which fade to pale green by flowering time.

HABITAT The Burnt Orchid, also known as the Burnt-tip Orchid, was once widespread throughout chalk and limestone grassland areas in England but it has undergone a severe decline and is now extinct in many counties. It can only survive in the shortest downland turf and is easily outcompeted by grasses and scrub.

WHERE TO LOOK Only a few scattered populations remain on the high chalk downlands of Hampshire, in the north. Sites include Martin Down (NNR), around the prominent Bokerley Dyke and the Meadow Clary site of Porton Down. The neighbouring county, Wiltshire remains a stronghold.

SIMILAR SPECIES

The Lady Orchid (p.54) is much larger and its lip is a different colour and shape.

Pyramidal Orchid
Anacamptis pyramidalis

FLOWERING TIME June to August

HEIGHT 45cm

DESCRIPTION With its densely packed, pyramid-shaped spikes of deep pink flowers, this orchid is easy to identify and found in all parts of the three counties with a calcareous bedrock. As the flowers open the shape of the spike changes from a pyramid to a globe. Each flower has one sepal and both petals that form a hood over a broad, deeply three-lobed lip and a long, thread-like spur. Pyramidal Orchid is pollinated by both day- and night-flying moths and butterflies. During daylight hours the vivid flowers attract visiting insects, by evening it is the increasingly strong, sweet and musky scent that lures in the night-flying moths. A sugary sap is contained within the walls of the spur which only an insect with a long proboscis can access. The slender, green stem has strap-shaped leaves at the base and much shorter, pointed leaves higher up the stem. Both the leaf and shoot survive the winter.

HABITAT This colourful species is locally common on chalk grassland throughout Hampshire and the Isle of Wight. It grows on dry, well-drained grassland on chalk or limestone. It can be found in large numbers in short and taller grass and also among scrub. It has the ability to rapidly recolonise new grassland and abandoned pasture including road verges, churchyards, old quarries and disused railway lines.

WHERE TO LOOK Central and eastern chalk downland of Hampshire and in the north-west around Highclere and Burghclere. Martin Down (NNR), Broughton Down, Noar Hill (HIWWT), Yew Hill (BC). It is the most common orchid to be found on the chalk hills of the Isle of Wight at Arreton, Compton and Tennyson Downs (all HIWWT).

DID YOU KNOW?

Pyramidal Orchid is the county flower of the Isle of Wight.

62

Green-winged Orchid

Anacamptis morio

STATUS Red Listing: Near Threatened

FLOWERING TIME Late April to mid-June

HEIGHT 8–30cm

DESCRIPTION This beautiful, petite orchid has a few large flowers which are very distinctive. Though they can vary in colour from deep red-purple to rose-pink or white, the sepals and petals form a hood clearly marked with green or bronze parallel veins. The broad lip is often violet-purple, whiter in the centre, and at the mouth of the spur there are usually purple spots and blotches. The flowers produce no nectar and the plant uses a powerful scent to trick bees, especially bumblebees, into visiting and cross-pollinating them. There is a rosette of leaves at ground level and the stem leaves, which are never spotted, closely clasp the stem.

HABITAT In the New Forest Green-winged orchids are locally distributed and not abundant. Elsewhere in Hampshire they are typically found in old pastures and gravel pits; on dry chalk-based grasslands, in damper clay meadows; and sand dunes. Since the 1950s agricultural changes, including the ploughing up of pastures and the use of fertilisers, have led to a dramatic fall in numbers and it is one of our most rapidly disappearing species.

WHERE TO LOOK A large colony of Green-winged Orchids blooms each year at Headley Gravel Pit in north Hampshire, however, access is restricted and a visitor permit is required from HIWWT. Lower Test (also HIWWT), Martin Down (NNR), Alice Holt Forest (Forestry Commission). Compton and Tennyson Downs on the Isle of Wight.

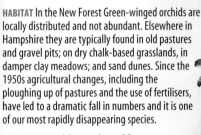

DID YOU KNOW?

Green-winged orchid flowers come in many shades of purple and in other colours too, from pink, white and even apricot.

Lizard Orchid

Himantoglossum hircinum

STATUS Red Listing: Vulnerable. Fully protected under Schedule 8 of the Wildlife and Countryside Act 1981.

FLOWERING TIME Early June to late July

HEIGHT Up to 75cm

DESCRIPTION The Lizard Orchid is our strangest-looking 'mimic' species. It is a large plant with tall spikes of straggly greyish-green flowers which resemble a maypole in action. On closer inspection each individual flower has the appearance of a lizard with the three-lobed lip resembling the long tail and back legs. In bud the central lobe is coiled like a clock spring which slowly unrolls to extend outwards, with several twists. The pale flowers are streaked or rimmed with brownish purple. They smell strongly of billy goat to attract pollinating insects. The stem is surrounded by large leaves which usually begin to wither when the plant is in flower. Plants can be long-lived (up to 19 years), but they may not flower every year.

HABITAT This orchid is on the edge of its range in England and its distribution and numbers fluctuate notoriously. It grows sporadically in well-drained, open, sunny spots on chalk and limestone grasslands among both closely-cropped and long grass..

WHERE TO LOOK The Lizard Orchid is very rare in the two counties with only occasional records of single plants. The last record was of one plant found in an Itchen valley water meadow, north-west of Winchester, in 1993.

DID YOU KNOW?

Lizard Orchid was thought to be extinct in 1900, then expanded rapidly in the warmer period between 1920 and 1940, then numbers began to fall again.

Fly Orchid

Ophrys insectifera

STATUS Red Listing: Vulnerable. On the Biodiversity Action Plan UK list of priority species.

FLOWERING TIME End of April to June

HEIGHT Up to 50cm

DESCRIPTION The Fly Orchid is a very distinctive species and is the most fascinating example of insect mimicry among British orchids. The tall, slender spikes have well-spaced flowers which resemble a group of small flies sitting on a stem. The folded dark-purple lip resembles an insect's hairy body and at the base of the lip there are two glistening 'eyes'. The slate-blue band across the centre forms the speculum and shines like folded wings. The column forms the insect's head and the two small brown petals the insect's antennae. Although the plant does not produce nectar, it releases a scent that mimics a female wasp's sexual pheromones. The scent, combined with the shape and velvety texture of the flowers prove irresistible to male digger wasps which attempt to mate with the flowers and inadvertently help to pollinate the plant. The narrow, strap-shaped, blue-green leaves emerge in autumn, lasting through the winter.

HABITAT The Fly Orchid can be found at the edge of beechwoods and chalk scrub on chalk and limestone soils. It prefers the better-lit areas in glades and along rides, as well as shaded road banks. Occasionally it will grow in shadier locations such as overgrown hazel coppice.

WHERE TO LOOK Chappetts Copse (HIWWT) and Old Winchester Hill (NNR), amongst the scrub. Old Burghclere Lime Quarry – a visitor permit is required from HIWWT.

DID YOU KNOW?

Fly Orchids, once widespread, have declined so rapidly that they are now listed as Vulnerable by the International Union for the Conservation of Nature.

Bee Orchid

Ophrys apifera

FLOWERING TIME Early June to late July

HEIGHT 10–45cm

DESCRIPTION One of our best known and well-loved orchids, this exotic-looking species resembles a fat, furry bumblebee perched on a stalk. Each inflorescence usually has two to seven flowers. The three large pink sepals contrast with the velvety maroon, pouch-like lip which is decorated with yellow markings and forms the 'body' of the bee. The two small side lobes are particularly hairy and resemble the bee's knees. The slender, greenish or pinkish-brown petals form the bee's 'antennae'. Bee Orchids can vary in colour, shape and markings – one example with a pointed lip is known as 'wasp orchid'. The flowers have evolved to attract male bees as pollinators, by luring them in to 'mate'. However, almost all plants are self-pollinated. Soon after the flower opens the anther releases the pollinia which dangle like little balls on the ends of their flexible stalks to be blown by a breeze onto the stigma. The pale green basal leaves appear in September to November and often look scorched by summer.

HABITAT Though the Bee Orchid has an aura of rarity it is an adaptable grassland species and can be found in large numbers across a wide variety of habitats, from well-drained calcareous grassland and disused gravel pits to roadside verges. It has even been known to pop up in garden lawns.

WHERE TO LOOK This species most often occurs on the chalk of central and eastern Hampshire. Sites include Martin Down, Farnborough Airfield, Portsdown Hill and Butser Hill (HCC), Yew Hill (BC), Noar Hill (HIWWT) and Old Winchester Hill (NNR). Tennyson Down and Compton Down on the Isle of Wight.

SIMILAR SPECIES

Early Spider-orchid (p.71) flowers in April and has yellowish sepals and petals, rather than pink, has a shiny slate blue band on its lip and lacks yellow markings.

Lesser Twayblade
Neottia cordata

FLOWERING TIME Mid-May to mid-August

HEIGHT 3–25cm

DESCRIPTION A smaller and more delicate version of
Common Twayblade. There are normally two apple-
green, heart-shaped leaves near the base of a
reddish, hairy stem. Each plant has up to 20
flowers. The petals are blunt and spreading,
usually copper in colour. The slender lip is
long and forked. A central channel in the
lip contains nectar which attracts
pollinating gnats and small flies.

HABITAT Wet moorland and bogs, often
in the shelter of heather.

WHERE TO LOOK Locally this orchid is
considered extinct. No genuine records
have been recorded since the 1970s,
when it was found at a single site
near Brockenhurst in the New Forest.

Summer Lady's-tresses
Spiranthes aestivalis

FLOWERING TIME Mid-July to mid-August

HEIGHT Up to 40cm

DESCRIPTION As its name suggests, Summer Lady's-tresses
flowers earlier than its more common cousin. It is also
distinguished by its taller stems and larger, whiter
flowers that are noticeably slimmer than those of
Autumn Lady's-tresses. Four to six narrow leaves
are clustered around its base, not to one side
as in the more common species.

HABITAT Wet, boggy conditions such as
marshes and wet heaths.

WHERE TO LOOK Historically Summer
Lady's-tresses has always been restricted
to the New Forest. The last proven
record was in the 1950s near Lyndhurst.
There were rumours of flowering in
1980, but these remain unproven. It is
officially declared extinct in Britain.

Northern Marsh-orchid
Dactylorhiza purpurella

FLOWERING TIME Mid-June to early July

HEIGHT 10–30cm

DESCRIPTION Typically it is a plant of northern Britain, as its name suggests. It has magenta-red flowers with a broad, diamond-shaped lip and dark markings. Flower spikes are square-topped in appearance. The four to six broad leaves are clustered towards the base of the stout stem, occasionally marked with small spots towards the tips.

HABITAT Fens, marshes and water meadows up to an altitude of 600m.

WHERE TO LOOK This orchid has not been seen at its former marshland site east of Southampton since 1986. However, one colony in the New Forest, thought to have died out, was rediscovered in 1999.

Early Spider-orchid
Ophrys spegodes

FLOWERING TIME Early April to end of May

HEIGHT 5–15cm

DESCRIPTION An insect mimic orchid, its large, brown and almost round lip resembles the body of a spider. Convex, velvety in texture and rich brown in colour, the lip has a shiny slate-grey mark shaped like the letter 'H' across the centre. The side lobes form two golden-brown furry humps like shoulders.

HABITAT Old flower-rich grassland on chalk and limestone.

WHERE TO LOOK This orchid has made sporadic appearances in Hampshire and the Isle of Wight in the last century. It was last seen in the western chalk on the Isle of Wight in the 1990s. Although it has officially been declared extinct in the two counties, it may yet be hidden, waiting to be rediscovered again.

Species index

Recommended books

The book with its 36 species mentioned is just an introduction to the orchids found in Hampshire &
the Isle of Wight. If you want to learn more then the following books are recommended.

Wild Orchids of Hampshire and the Isle of Wight (1995) by Martin N. Jenkinson. Published by Orchid
Sundries Ltd. ISBN 1 873035 03 9 (paperback) – a more specialist publication with distribution maps
and colour plates.

Britain's Orchids (2004) by David Lang. Published by Wild Guides. ISBN 1 903657 067 (hardcover) – a
simple-to-use full colour guide. A contribution from the sale of this book goes to The Wildlife Trusts.

Orchids of Britain and Ireland (2nd edition 2009) by Ann and Simon Harrap. Published by A & C Black
Publishers Ltd. ISBN-10: 1408105713 – a comprehensive guide with beautiful photography.